Dear
Friend

Dear
Friend

Julie Ann Stine

AUGSBURG Publishing House • Minneapolis

To Ella and Emil Hanson,
parents who are loving and loved

Contents

Dear friend,

This collection of reflections and prayers is the result of years of knowing a Friend who is comforter, confessor, confidant—one who knows my being as a person, as a woman, who understands struggle and pain, who rejoices in strength and celebrates joy, who enters into doubts and questioning, who forgives freely and loves unreservedly.

My hope is that these lines articulate our bond with the uncommon Friend who moves with us in the dailiness of living and who supports us in our joys, struggles, doubts, and questions with a resounding "yes" to life!

May God bless our togetherness and friendship as we move increasingly toward such awareness of our dear Friend.

Julie Ann Stine

The lost coin
was retrieved
from its dark corner
and the woman
rejoiced with
her friends.

The lost sheep
was found
in its wandering
and the shepherd
carried it home
with gladness.

The lost son
returned from
a far country
and his father
gave thanks
with a feast.

There is joy
in finding
but greater joy
in being found.

I'm glad you found me

I'm glad you found me, Lord, because nothing is so lonely as being lost. Thank you for keeping me yours and holding me safe in your care. Knowing that I am yours and that my home is with you gives me a sense of real belonging.

Sometimes I forget, though, and need to be reminded where I belong. Thank you for sending people to remind me and for giving me a nudge yourself. Amen.

Some are beggars
on God's threshold
for a handout of
    mercy
    love
    healing
and any fringe benefit
he may confer.

Legal tender

I do not choose
the giving
but the Giver
so I am not relegated
to pounding the gates
of heaven for a favor
    but in that choice
    I place myself
    squarely in his service
    with all my needs
    to fill.

I need not beg
for his abundance
    and he need not beg
    for my commitment.

Our contract
is not legal bond
    but sealed forever
    on a cross.

Show me ways of service, Lord. Open new doors for
me and shut some old ones if you think they're better
closed. I do not have the wisdom to decide about
those old doors. I need your hand on the knob.

Thank you for this day and for the knowledge that you
are always with me, supplying every need. Amen.

David was
a shepherd boy
turned king
   but only when
   he left the hills
   to join a battle.

To choose
a cause

The quiet field
of grazing sheep
could not unleash
his power
   and God needed
   the man David
   for Israel's future
so he called the boy
to meet a giant
on a crucial day
   in preparation
   for the man
   he would become.

David proved himself
a warrior
for the Lord.

I too would leave
the safety
of my field
   if I could only know
   which battle to choose.

   I'm confused, Lord. There are too many banners flying,
too many causes going, too many empty cups to fill.
Where shall I go first? What shall I do first? Shall I head
a parade or march in the ranks? I must stand quietly
before you and listen before jumping on the bandwagon.
But let me know, Lord, or I may end up in the
wrong uniform. Amen.

Zacchaeus
was too small
to see Jesus
until he climbed a tree
to bring him nearer.

I am at times
too small
to see my Lord
   until I mount a plane
   whose soaring wingtips
   span the galaxies
   or climb a hillside
   and view a sunset
   splashed against
   the skyline
   or raise my eyes
   to look into
   the face of my
   most earthly love—
and suddenly my Lord
has moved very near.

I am too small

Let me remember, Lord, to see your touch on sunsets and hillsides and sky. But let me also remember to see you in my home, in my family. For this is where I do my living, and this is where I need you most of all.

But oh! I need to climb higher on some days to see! Amen.

Jesus used a whip
to drive pious profiteers
from the temple
and turned the tables
on their own deceit
in one swift moment
of his anger.

I need to change

He uses conscience
to purge
pious peripheries
from my life
and drive out
the litter
that strangles
a clean worship.

I am mindful
that I too
would rather
change money
    than change me.

God, I need your righteous indignation in my life so
that I don't become so encumbered with serving the
church that I forget about serving you. It's easier to
change the altar linens than to change my heart—and I
know I need to change its arrogance, pride, hate, and
jealousy. But I'm scared, Lord, because I know there's so
much to change and I might not be ready.

Help me know what to change first and then be ready
for it—because I know you are a powerhouse of
action! Amen.

One brother ran away
to some far country
where he lived it up
with lush women
and a few
ill-chosen friends.

Prodigal stay-at-home

But he came home again—
more glad than ever
for a father
who was waiting
and a love
that surprised him.

The other stayed home
with swollen pride
and pompous indignation
to mind his manners
and his father's flocks.

His far country
had familiar boundaries
of jealousy
and smoldering resentment.

He couldn't run home
to his father
for the waiting love
because he thought
he'd never been away.

How can I duck a lesson such as this parable, Lord?
I've been that prodigal son—running from responsibilities
and issues right in my neighborhood, hiding behind
vague generalities when you wanted me to face specifics.

I didn't sign that petition that came around to keep a
black family from our block. But neither did I go out
and try to change minds. I didn't slander the woman in

my church who hurts so many of us with words, but neither have I the courage to face her with a reconciliation, nor am I willing to bear the burden of her spiteful unhappiness.

I hate conflict and argument, so I keep silent when I should speak out. On the other hand, words tumble out in profusion when I should keep still. I'm a vast succession of paradoxes that there isn't time to sort out. So I come running home to you, Lord, over and over again. And you keep welcoming me back with open arms and a feast.

But I'm also the brother who stayed home. I'm ashamed when I feel smug self-importance over playing the martyr. This kind of prodigal is much more respectable, though, so I can talk myself into feeling justified. And I'm never so arrogant as when I feel justified. But don't let me get away with it, Lord. Make me sensitive to my actions—and the reasons for them. Amen.

The question
was an honest one
from a man
who had kept
the commandments
and also his possessions
intact:
  "Good Teacher,
  what must I do
  to receive eternal life?"

Rich and honest

The answer
was no less honest:
"Give everything away
and follow me,"
Jesus said,
  seeing that the man
  had much to give
  except himself.

The rich man turned away.
Perhaps he never again
touched so closely to the truth.

I wonder if a yearning
gripped his soul
when he remembered
the invitation he refused
  and if he
  ever turned
  to open the door
  he had closed
  himself.

O God, help me to discern your invitation, wherever
it may occur. Help me to walk through the open doors of
opportunities you place before me. Embolden me to
take risks if needed. I don't want to fall on my face,

Lord, but I know that may be part of risk taking, and it won't hurt anything but my pride. Let me be willing to fail without worrying about a damaged ego or my inflatable image.

I, who have everything, need to learn to give myself . . . to people, to causes, to you. Amen.

Jacob matched his strength
against the Lord
in the long night
of his struggle.

Decision making

In the morning
he was neither
winner nor loser
richer nor poorer
   but stronger
   for his wrestling
   in the night
and able to march
in time with
the drumbeat
of God.

I would hear
the beat of drums
into my day
but first
   a time for wrestling
   in the night.

   I am so often trying to jump the gun, God, on
important decisions, rushing into my deadline before
taking time to pray it through. The bigger the decision,
the more it seems I try to hurry it along and get it
over with. Let me learn to take time to listen to you,
God—*take time to listen*—rather than batting the breeze
before you in a panic of indecision.
   Help me control my thinking and my time until I
can come before you with clear consciousness of my
direction and hear your marching orders. Amen.

21

Pioneering

Abraham
turned his back
upon a familiar past
and stepped forward
into an unknown future.

I wonder
if he went
with singing
    or with a certain
    trepidation.

I wonder
whether Sarah
packed her grip
without a gripe
or if she
    did some shouting
    and some weeping
    before takeoff.

Her voice
went unheard
    if she shouted
and her tears
went unseen
    if she wept
for Abraham
had his marching orders
and was listening
for the first downbeat
from God.

But Sarah
with her wit
and beauty
followed—
    and it will be
    forever to her credit

that she pioneered a frontier
to the Promised Land
and mothered
its descendants
into being.

You haven't called me into a new land, Lord, yet you've
called me into new places in the same familiar territory.
Let me see newness in old places, and then may I have
the courage of an Abraham and Sarah to move for you.
Help me to keep my bags packed, Lord, and then to
perceive the moment of departure. Amen.

No bargain

Esau was not
all that bad
   only hungrier
   for food
   he could eat
than for a birthright
of undernourished words.

He sold out
for soup.

Jacob was not
all that good
   he was an opportunist
   in sheep's clothing
who played upon
his brother's
weakness
   and his father's
   blindness
with his mother's
help.

He bought up
when the stock
was low.

It might have been
fair trade
   but Jacob struck
   a dishonorable bargain
and ended up
with all those Israelites
to lead!

I'm sometimes surprised by your choices, Lord. I will
remind myself today that my inner person is for you to
use. Neither Esau nor Jacob was a great person, yet

25

you were able to use Jacob—a conniver, a cheater—and fashion him to your purposes. And what high purposes they were! What an impact this man Jacob made for you!

My people-perceptions are dulled so often, Lord. Awaken in me the awareness of potential in others, and help me tap the resources I find. Amen.

Hannah's bargaining with God
was not without consequence
   and her firstborn
   became a temple ward
   and errand boy
   for old Eli.

Hannah

Samuel's little coat
became a symbol of her pilgrimage.
She wove into it her love
to warm him against temple stone
as her mother-arms could not.

But Eli had to deal with
adolescent fears
and hot awakenings of flesh!

I wonder if Samuel
harbored some misgivings
on the prayer
which landed him so surely
on the temple doorstep
in a priestly procession
from which there was
no turning back
or if at times
he dreamt of
playing leapfrog
on the old sandlot
with siblings
for whose appearance
his mother
did not find it necessary
to negotiate.

   Lord, sometimes I feel trapped, going dead center in
the direction mapped out for me by birth, circumstance,
heritage. Maybe that's how Samuel felt at times. Yet I

know I can alter my direction, with your help. I am free to change. It's much easier to blame my genes than set about the job of rehabilitation or reconciliation. Help me take a good look at my life, then do something about it! Amen.

Jesus was an artist with words.
He gave no pat answers
to questions posed for him.

"Is it right
to pay taxes?"
   they asked
   and he answered,
"Pay to the emperor
and to God
what belongs
to each of them."

Tax problem

Herein lies my problem—
   deciding which
   is which
   and to whom
   goes what
   and when!

The government
has affixed its
own tax deadline
   but to my knowledge
   God has not done
   likewise.

Due dates
and deadlines
are not for him
   but he has declared
   high interest rates
   for anyone who chooses
   to borrow carelessly
   and the return investment
   is great for those
   who dare to risk
   a stockholder's share
   in eternity!

I never seem to have enough money to go around for taxes, Lord. At times I even resent having to pay them. Yet I know mine is the privilege of living in a bountiful and free country that needs my support in every way. Thank you for a country in which there is freedom and opportunity. Help me to be a positive force for its improvement when I can. Amen.

The request
was very simple—
   that his disciples
   wash the feet of others
   as Jesus washed theirs—
but they were
properly indignant
on both counts.

Help me serve

Through the years
God also asks my presence
at that ceremony
and presents me
with a similar request.

I am uncomfortable
   for to my great surprise
   I find knees
   that will not bend
   and a mind
   that resists.

Washing feet is dirty business—
   being clobbered
   for messing in
   a private life,
   being called names
   for untying shoelaces
   and pulling off socks
   when chief priorities
   are my own clean feet
   and my own clean hands
   without blemish.

Maybe he didn't mean
grandstand dramatics—
   maybe it's enough
   to take the hand
   of someone who needs help.

Hand holding
is far safer
than foot washing—
    and cleaner too!

That simple request
is not simple
    but it stands
    without shame
    unimpressed with
    arthritic knees
    or uptight minds.

The request still stands
at a point in history
and before me—
    before me.

I'm tired of the nursing home smell, God, and I don't
feel much like playing checkers with Old Jake once a
month, or trying to talk Eva into coming out of her
room for a while. The rest of them are mostly senile and
hardly know I'm there, except Katy, who smiles
sometimes, and Bertha, who speaks German and doesn't
know I can't understand a word.

I don't think I'm getting through to my little kid in
the tutoring program either. He doesn't read any better
than he did two months ago. But he wants to make
sure I'm there every week and can't wait to start jabbering
to fill up the hour. Sometimes I wonder if it's worth it.
(Then I remember the times he runs up and grabs my
hand in his grubby little fist.)

I've had to fill in twice lately to serve at church, and
I'm fed up with rushing to bake bars or prepare a
last-minute devotional to replace someone who probably
just wouldn't make the extra effort. Bailing people out
of a crisis isn't my idea of service. I'd rather be on a
missionary field. (No, I wouldn't.)

Why am I so discouraged? Serving is dirty business at times, and I don't like to be dirty. God, help me to see you there in the nursing home, in the tutoring program, even in my church, where I should see you most of all.

Forgive me for complaining. I didn't really expect that being a Christian would be easy . . . just easier. Amen.

It is not enough
to reach a hand
to my black sister
in the ghetto
   when my mind
   is barred and shuttered
   in a ghetto of its own.

Get me out of here!

I try at times
to climb the barricade
and when I do
I can perceive a love
   that crumbles walls.

It is not enough
to care a little
for her—
   I need her
   caring a little
   for me—
enough to lift me
from a prisoned mind
just as I would free her
from closed housing.

Maybe we can both
destroy the ghetto
for each other.

I didn't know there were so many kinds of ghettos
until I started climbing walls over which I couldn't see.
God, help me to admit prejudice when I have it and to
knock down its walls when possible so that I can be
about your business of building a kingdom. Please, God,
crumble my walls! Amen.

Mary sat
at the feet of Jesus
and listened with
her heart and mind—
  loving her Lord.

Martha hastened
to make ready
for the comfort
of her guest—
  loving her Lord.

The better choice

It became
a question of priority—
  and Jesus
  made it clear
  that Mary
  had her values
  in right order.

But it was Martha
whose quick hands
and warm efficiency
  gave Mary the freedom
  to sit for a time
  at his feet.

Dear God, I'd rather be a Mary than a Martha, but not always for the right reasons. I like to meditate (if I can find some quiet time), read the Bible, go to church, attend retreats. But my temptation is to immerse myself in these to the detriment of my family.

I need to be more of a Martha and keep a shining home full of hospitality and good food, as well as a Mary, open to new ideas and good books.

Help me to keep a well-balanced life so that I can discern each day where my priorities will be, and then to change my schedule if necessary. Amen.

She poured her devotion
from the alabaster jar
on the feet of Jesus
and her tears and perfume
rose in lavish adoration
of her Lord.

Protocol was not observed
in that act of worship
but the beauty of it
has lived for centuries.

He looked at her
and loved her
    and the fragrance
    of her offering
    lifted his tiredness
and her ready gift
was music
against a monotone
of words
that day.

Together
they celebrated!
She brought her past
    and the need
    to be forgiven.
He brought his love
    and the need
    to make whole.

They both left the feast
of celebration
richer for each other.

Who is to say
which need
was the greater?

Let's celebrate

I'm lifted in happiness, God, and need to share it with someone. Will you listen? I've been especially aware of my family today and of the love we have for each other. Thank you for forgiving our selfish mistakes and for blessing our togetherness. We're a volatile, alive bunch, Lord, and need your steadying arm.

I'm also newly grateful for our friends, who show their loyalty and love in big and little ways. Help me think of ways to let them understand how dear they are— maybe a note of gratitude, a phone call, an invitation to dinner.

There's so much good in the world, Lord. I'm glad to be alive and to know it. Let the perfume of my joy spill over more often on others. Thank you for my life! Amen.

Moses had eyes to see
a burning bush
and ears to hear
the voice of God
calling him to work
he did not relish.

Averse at first

He was not slow
to speak
his lack of eloquence
    and well
    did he proclaim
    his quick
    reluctance
    to be called
    by God.

Moses had eyes and ears
    but not much stomach
    for the wilderness ahead.

He must have been
mightily persuaded!
At times I want
the burning bushes
of my life
to be dissolved
in ash
    but God speaks
    over my reluctance
and leads me
from a cozy Midian
into a wilderness
    and from my
    safe perimeter
    holds me to
    a steep and rugged trail.
I have been
mightily persuaded!

39

I'm a coward, Lord, and want to be absolved from confrontation. But you seem to be pushing me into it. Give me strength, then, to handle the day you have given and to be wiser at the end of it than I was at the beginning. Amen.

Leftovers

The Temple treasury
was being filled
with leftovers
when the widow came
and gave all she had.

The rich men
must have squirmed a bit
when Jesus rated hers
the best gift
   for perhaps they knew
   they must take on
   her support
   from that moment.

Their indignation
can be tolerated
in view of the economy.

I am neither rich
nor poor
nor widowed
   and my life is filled
   with abundant leftovers
   I try to recycle
   into the economy
with Goodwill bags
by the score
or fall clothing drives
that help clean closets.
Occasionally I add
to the leftovers
a brand-new dress
that didn't fit.
(My benevolence
is overwhelming.)

Jesus was not
thinking of economy

41

when he praised the widow—
   only of her generous spirit
   of giving, and giving, and giving
without pious reminders
to balance the budget
or make the house payment
in the name of good business.

I would be
a lavish middle-class spendthrift
for the Lord
   (if only I can forget
   how much I've already spent).

   There are times to be frugal, Lord, and penny-pinching, and cautious, but right now I can't think when. Right now the needs from your children are crying louder than my budget, and I remind myself of the new drapes in our living room and feel guilty.

   Why do I quibble over pennies when you are needing dollars? Help me to stop quibbling and to sort out the garbage from real needs. Help me to become a real spendthrift when it comes to your work and miserly when it comes to me. That's the only way I can balance my budget. Amen.

The paralytic rose
from his bed
and walked away
when Jesus said,
    "Rise and walk."

My paralysis
is of the spirit
and is set free
by God's forgiveness:
    "Take heart, my son;
    your sins are forgiven."

Some days it is not easy
to hear those words
and know that forgiveness
and feel the power
that sets me free.

Some days I carry
my bed around with me
like the paralytic
    but unlike him
I'm unwilling to let it go
and walk away free!

I'm selfish about my sins, Lord, and at times I want to
hold them close. It's as though I want something to hang
onto, something to call my very own. Nobody's sins are
quite like mine—thank goodness.

Forgive my lack of maturity. Like the paralytic, I'm
mesmerized in myself. I stumble around in sins without
the will to let go. Help me to grow in believing that I
might place my burdens on you with full assurance of
your forgiveness. Set me free of myself, Lord. Amen.

43

Joy is where
the action is
   and the action
   was the wedding
   and good friends
   gathered to celebrate
   at Cana of Galilee.

Joy

Joy is where
God is actively
present in a life
   and where friends
   can gather
   to toast an occasion.

Miracles
are very present
   and God
   is very near
   to the joyous ones.

Dear God, thank you for people, parties, fun, for reasons to celebrate with friends, for time to "let our hair down" and be glad with one another. Our islands of happy times make precious memories and I'm very conscious of storing memories against a future need. Amen.

Paul of Tarsus
found himself that night
beneath a desert sky
   and armies
   could not quell
   the zeal in him.

Lately come

The Christ
had never such
a messenger
   to run abroad
   and tell of him.
He who blundered
with Pharisaic eloquence
before his God
   now leaped
   to make amends
and wept in adoration
of the one
who would not
let him go.

The Christ
had never such
a messenger
   to run abroad
   and tell of him.

That brash philanderer Paul finally found you, God, and admitted to a Christ. What a great follower he became! I found you earlier in life than he, but my life hasn't shown nearly the results. Perhaps the zeal in me has settled for a slow leak of faith until there are days I can't even pump up enough enthusiasm to get it off the ground. I wonder if your Paul ever had to work at enthusiasm and had a pumping job to do.

Thank you for a Paul. Thanks for my life, too, which can be its own kind of messenger in your name. Amen.

Thomas doubted
what he heard
about the living Lord
   until he stood in his presence
   and touched his scars.

Jesus used his doubt
to whet a growing
edge of faith
   and took the risk
   of confrontation.

I want at times
a God to see
and touch
and am not
wholly satisfied
with spirit.

The earthy
finite part of me
requires substance
   so he gives to me
   my brother's scars
   to heal
   and my sister's grief
   to share
and in the clasp of hands
I touch my Lord.

What's it all about?

   Thank you for showing me a Thomas who could doubt
through his faith and come out on top. I am grateful for
the freedom of thought and deliberation, and for
knowing you are there waiting for me to come through.
   I seem to be stronger each time I struggle, Lord, and
that's encouraging. Thanks for not deserting! Amen.

47

My lamp is lit
and shining
and throws its beams
in darkened corners
of the room
    but the flame
    flickers
    and falters
    and fades
in the wind-tossed night.

In turbulence
it does not sustain
its little flame.

How can I
light the world
when I have trouble lighting
one small room?

My faltering light

God, help me to trim the wick of my lamp that it may burn a steady flame and not be snuffed out by every draft that sweeps through. I live in a drafty world. Help me to discipline my mind and body to take off the frayed edges and to be wholly yours. Help me to live so that you will shine through words and actions and so that your love can make a difference to someone else in a night of living. Amen.

Encounter

The woman came
to draw water at the well
and found instead
the Lord.

Her Samaritan conscience
questioned such a rabbi Jew
in conversation with a prostitute
    but her heart cried out
    for such a one
    and cared little
    whether words
    were circumspect.

Jesus cared
    and held her gently
    with his words
    until her past and present
    shone with clarity.

She shed her past
in a confession
    and risked a life
    of new dimension
    without leaving town.

The woman of Samaria
had an encounter with God—
    reason enough
    for stopping
    in the heat of day
    for water and
    a fresh beginning.

I'm reaching out to you, God, in the hours of the
morning when I stagger awake, greedy for more sleep,
and hardly conscious until that first cup of coffee.
When fully awake I'm caught in the rush of the

noontime, whether at work on a lunch hour or at home with the kids. I reach again past the clamor with only half a mind (the other half is occupied with peanut butter and jelly sandwiches).

My encounter with you is fragmented, God, into bits and pieces from my day. But how terrible it would be not to know you are there when I come with those bits and pieces.

The woman of Samaria must have been thrilled to unsuspectingly find you at her well. Please stay at my well, too, because I need many drinks from your living water through my day. Amen.

I wonder if Peter
was surprised
to find the words
so ready on his tongue,
turning away suspicion—
   "I never knew him."

Conscience-stricken

The Lord knew Peter
better than
he knew himself
and had prepared him
for the bitter knowing.

But it made his grief
the sharper
and the final reality
of his lie
more painful.

With or without
the crowing cock
his conscience
would have winced
as he remembered
the brave promise
to be faithful.

He turned away
and wept.

Bravo! for a Peter
with tears to weep
over the fresh sorrow
of himself
and for a Christ
who already knew
   and loved him still.

I'm grateful for knowing of Peter, Lord, for in him I find a reflection of my weaknesses and I know you loved him in spite of them. Thank you for this reassurance. You know me better than I know myself—brave words and a coward's heart, strong resolutions and weak followup, much criticism and little praise.

Let me never hold back the tears of remorse that will make me clean, because you have told me that I can be forgiven again and again.

Let me stand clean before you, Lord, and thank you. Amen.

No loitering

"No Loitering" signs
hadn't been posted
for a while
and the cripple
sat at the pool's edge
waiting for the
magic plunge.

Thirty-eight years
with no action
is long to wait.

Jesus saw the
crippled spirit
and challenged
its procrastination—
    "Will you be healed?"

The cripple dodged
the answer and
pointed an accusing finger
at his peers
who had not scrambled
on his behalf.

But Jesus would
have none of it.
He posted his "No Loitering"
by raising him on sturdy legs
and sending him
on his way.

I am loitering at the pool of my life, Lord, with all the
right answers and rationale to support my procrastination.
Give me the courage to plunge into my life's pool—even
without the guarantee that I will surface. But stay with
me, Lord. It's scary to be fully responsible for who I am.
Amen.

Death
is swinging wide
the door into
a new day
    not with regrets
    and old fears
but with a fresh
song to sing
upon the morning
and the warm smile
of friends who
greet us there.

Death
is as sudden
as the last
heartbeat
and as bright
as the first
hello.

Death
is only a word
that means
we have stepped
into another
daytime of
living.

Death is hello

Most of us run scared, Lord, in the face of death. We're
so enamored of the world we know that we back off
from one that is unfamiliar. Thank you for the assurance
of the new beginning you will have for us. I know you
will be waiting to say hello. Amen.

Daniel stood alone
in a den of lions
knowing God was there
   and rising
   to the strength
   of that reality.

I am the prey

No whimpering for him!
   Instead the unabashed conviction
   that God rose supreme
   and deserved top priority.

I am astonished to discover
padded footprints of doubt
stalking my carpeted den
well-lined with books
   and confounded
   to perceive
   I am the prey.

My mind is vulnerable
and open to attack
without the stature
of a Daniel
   whose confidence
   was wholly in the Lord
and whose protection
was the steady
flame of faith.

   Lord, you know my quick and curious mind and
how intrigued I am with new ideas. You know how I love
a well-turned phrase and how thrilled I am
with word power.
   Help me to discern your value system as against
a comfortable philosophy. In a maze of books and
periodicals, let me not forget the Bible as the whetstone
of my mind and the bedrock of my faith. Amen.

A priest saw the need
and passed by.
    The gutters of life were not for him
    nor was he ready to stoop so low
    that his hand could touch a brother
    and lift him from the dust.

His indifference was shocking!
    Was he not
    in the business of the Lord
    and were not the synagogue fathers
    paying him well to stoop a little?

But who am I to be so shocked?
    My priestly function is at times
    inflated into incredible pride
    and with a sweeping arrogance
    I too have turned away from need
    on the other side of town.

And what of the Levite,
    smug with his religious fervor
    and busy keeping candles lit
    and incense burning?
    There was no time in that
    well-scheduled life
    for stopping on a grimy road.
    Roads were meant for travel
    and he had to keep moving.

Poor Levite, who did not hear
God calling him that day.
    And I am poor—who run
    to committees and subcommittees
    and consider agendas
    with a vast idea of my importance
    but who cannot hear God
    within a quiet heart.

Willing to be willing

Then the Samaritan—
    the looked-down-upon
    and unloved half-breed
    who came without a pedigree
    on which to hang his worth
    but who had a certain love
    to share with a man
    there in the dust.

That's for me!—
    that unsophisticated Samaritan
    with the guts to stop
    in a cluttered day
    to take the hand
    of a brother,
    that foolish Samaritan
    who didn't know
    how much time
    he was losing from his week,
    who didn't stop to tally
    the cost of his concern.
That's for me!

(But why is it I see myself
    more clearly in the other two?)

    I still wonder who my neighbor is at times, Lord, and
how far I must go in serving. I ask all the right questions,
but don't much care for the answers you hand back.
It's right from the shoulder with you, God, and it's
a bit disconcerting.
    The second mile, the other cheek, the coat off my back,
forgiveness from my heart—endless and unlimited.
There are so many neighbors. I feel helpless against the
millions who need food and clothing and homes.
I'm just a drop of water in a vast ocean of need!
    But I am one person, and my family makes us five.
Five people out looking for a neighbor. The new mother

58

in our block who isn't strong enough yet to manage—
maybe a hot dish is a beginning at least, until we
get used to the idea of looking around.

Give us the initiative, Lord, to get out and do a little
looking for a neighbor. Then, when we've found one,
help us to be willing to be willing. Amen.

Lot's wife
took one more look behind
and it became her last.
   (She was consumed
   with curiosity.)

**A time
for
looking back**

I understand Lot's wife
far better than
I will admit
   but know that
   I must risk
   the backward glance
because I find
in retrospect
a clear line
   showing distances
   I have already
   traveled.

A hand
to the ploughshare
does not deny
a mind
   that measures
   spirit growth.

   Today is a looking-back time, Lord, because I must
somehow see where I've been as clearly as where I'm
going. I can measure spirit growth that way—but
sometimes I'm embarrassed at what I see. I want to find
great strides of growth—greater compassion, understanding, tolerance. What I see are little spurts ahead and
a great deal of lagging, a few strong steps and lots of slow
shuffling. Yet, there *is* a little growth. Slowly but surely
there *is* a little more commitment and purpose. Hurrah!
for that little, and may I have the sense to rejoice over the
small steps without always looking for the great leaps.
Amen.

The crowds
followed Jesus
with parched souls
and hungry bodies
    and found that he
    could fill their stomachs
    as well as quench
    the spirit thirst.

How strange
that they declared
the fish and loaves
a miracle
    but scarcely saw
    the brimming souls
    that overflowed
    with new vitality.

The continuing
miracle of Jesus
was his quiet caring
and a shining love
that waited to penetrate
their blindness.

I think I am
too preoccupied
with fish and loaves
    to notice
    the brimming miracle
    of God in me.

Feeding the five thousand

Life is a never-ending meal preparation, God, and at
times I'd like to junk the whole business in favor of a
more sophisticated pursuit, such as reading the current
best seller or a book of the Bible, or even the luxury of
listening to the symphony orchestra—in person.
  The feeding of the five thousand must have been a

drudgery in your day too, God, and yet a miracle happened on that day. I need to see the miracles in my home, Lord, in the faces of my family, and not only see the dishes heaped with food.

Help me to see! Amen.

Judas kissed the Lord
 and turned
 a clean friendship
 into a soiled
 transaction.

History calls it
 betrayal.

Maybe it was more
 a matter of Jesus being
 too much man
 and too much God
 to tolerate in one
 Judas lifetime.

I think we
sell out too—
 in posh nightclubs
 over the fifth drink
 in legal hiding
 behind the fifth amendment
 in suburban churches
 by calling names
 and sticking tidy labels
 on our failures.

Judas lived and died
 a swift regret
 for such a kiss.

We live and die
our own regrets
 alone at night
 when we are stripped
 of our defenses
 and must face
 our own betrayals.

Personal pollution

Is Jesus still
    too much man
    and too much God
    to tolerate in
    one lifetime?

I'm ashamed of myself, God. I didn't have to pass on
that candid observation (otherwise known as gossip),
but I did. I didn't have to keep silent when my neighbor
was leveled at the coffee party, but I did. I didn't have
to sail out of church with my head in the air because
Jane didn't agree with me on integration, but I did.
I get so mad at narrow and bigoted people that I can
hardly wait to call them narrow and bigoted. I think then
I feel better, but I don't. I'm miserable because I close
the door on other people by my resentments.

Help me keep an open heart toward others with whom
I don't agree, and let the warmth of your love surround
me. Keep me honest with myself and with others,
but not so honest that I intentionally hurt someone.

I feel polluted, Lord, with my own ambiguities and
weaknesses, which I can see all too clearly against
your teaching and your love. Amen.

Low ebb

The yeast
raises the bread
ferments the wine
    and causes
    great things
    to happen.

The burst
of energy
activates.

The yeast
of my life
is deactivated.
    My spirit
    does not soar
and my lips
do not sing
    and my feet
    do not dance
but oh!
    how my mind
    thinks!

Help me, Lord, and energize this sagging spirit into a
vital life for some good on this blue-mood day.
Thanks. Amen.

Compassion
is an outpouring
of love
on the hurts
and scars
and ugliness
around us.

Necessary motive

Forgiveness
is an outpouring
of love
on the misdeeds
and hates
and bitterness
against us.

I need both
to such degree!
There is no end
of giving
I must do
    for the measure
    I confer
    will also be
    the measure returned
    to me.

I don't think I can forgive as I know I'm forgiven, Lord,
and it bothers me. I need so much of it from you and
others. I'm dragging my feet about the business of
forgiving and I pile up excuses why I can't.

Oh, I know what you say, Lord: "Forgive our trespasses
as we forgive those who trespass against us." My motive
in forgiving others is not pure, but necessary. Thank you
for loving my unloveliness, and show me how to forgive
in greater measure. Help me to forgive so that I don't
harbor resentments and can turn my energies to
better use. Amen.

Jesus performed
    a long-distance healing
    for the government man
    who had a long-distance faith
    and who considered it
    well within a day's work
    to petition the power
    of God.

Jesus even marveled
    that he perceived
    from the fringe crowd
    the core of his reality
    and was astute enough
    to draw on it.

Small wonder
    that it pleased him—
    when his own twelve
    were slow to such
    acknowledgement.

My little faith

    I seem to need so much proof that you hear me, God—
proof that you hear my prayers and will answer them,
that you approve of what I do (or at least, sometimes).
The centurion was smart enough to know you were for
real, and he acted on his realization. You must have been
very pleased and grateful.

    Forgive me for pounding on your door. I know it
isn't necessary. A gentle knock will do, or even a whisper
of thought. But sometimes I become frantic and want to
make sure you know my need.

    Thank you for being within reach whenever I need you,
which is always. Amen.

The good Pharisee
stood before Jesus
with his
    impeccable credentials
    important following   **Credit rating**
    imposing character
and his curious mind
pressed for answers
from the Rabbi.

"You must be born again
of the spirit," Jesus said,
    confounding Nicodemus
    with the proposition that
    high morality
    good ethics
    neighborliness
    were not enough
but that they might be
a good beginning
for an inner change
that whispers to the heart
as softly as a gentle wind
    but has the power
    to blow a mighty gale.

I think this Pharisee
made more than a beginning
and even helped to bury
the crucified body of his Friend
one day in Joseph's garden.

The tenderness
of such an act
tells me that
    the gentle wind had moved
    into a mighty gale
    and changed that
    Pharisaic heart.

69

Lord, I worry over my credit rating and keep track of my charge accounts so I can be a citizen of good standing in this community. But I wonder if I care enough about the rating I have with you. Do I spend enough time listening to you?

I'm half afraid that if I really listen I might have to do an about-face and see through different eyes. I'm afraid you might confront me with myself as you did Nicodemus. The mighty gale of the Spirit might even sweep me off my feet and I might have hard landing.

Help me not to be afraid to be born of the Spirit, God, because it's your Spirit and, after all, I'm yours. Whatever direction you move me, I'll go. But push hard. Sometimes I need a mighty gale! Amen.

Final test

Abraham complied
with God's fearful request
   that he prepare
   his only son
   as a burning sacrifice.

Isaac must have wondered
what the fuss was all about
   until the final moment
   when he knew.

I too have wondered
at the rigid test
imposed on Abraham
by God
   in using
   the old pagan custom
   of killing the firstborn
and whether Abraham
was filled with
doubts and questions
as he made grim preparation.

Old Abraham
came through
with flying colors—
   not so the
   ram caught
   in the thicket.

My little faith
would not stand
up to such a test
   and I would
   shout before
   the gates
   of heaven
   and wait for
   God to rescind

a demand
for which
there appeared
no purpose.

Each generation
gives its firstborn
sons as sacrifice
upon the altar
of a burning war.

My only marvel is
that we prepare
them with our love
and send them off
to hate
    and scarcely
    remember
    to shout before
    the gates
    of heaven.

I could not pass such a final test, Lord, and hope you
will not require it of me. I could not sacrifice a child of
mine upon your altar, for any reason. Yet some of my
friends have sent sons off to war. Maybe some of them
were willing, but most of them were not, Lord, and my
heart aches for their loss. Killing each other seems such a
childish way to settle differences or prove power. Help us
to grow in understanding, Lord, that such sacrifice will be
unnecessary. Let me prove my love for you and love for
my country—another way. Amen.

She was taken
in adultery
they said
   and so became
   the victim
   of their scorn
   and fair target
   for the stones
   they planned to hurl
   from their heights
   of indignation.
"Let him who is without sin
among you cast the first stone,"
Jesus said,
   and in the awkward silence
   each man turned away
   until no one was left.

It turned out to be
a quiet day after all.

I wonder if her
partner in the act
had pleaded innocent
or only walked out the back door
without loss of stature
or fear of reprisal.

Where were *his* accusers?

History isn't written
by telling all the truth
   for then the story
   might have read,
   "man caught in adultery"
   and maybe never
   would have reached
   a first edition
   anywhere.

Fallen woman

God, I've done it again. I've looked at that woman and felt good that I am not that great a sinner. I felt good that I am better than she! What gives me the right to decide that? What gives me the right to measure someone else's mistakes and sweep my own under the rug?

I am grateful to be a woman and proud of the functions of my body in the act of love. It's a beautiful part of your created order. Thank you. Let me be mindful of the women to whom this beauty is denied.

Let me be aware of the temptation to measure sins according to my yardstick instead of yours. You measure depth of spirit and I just measure yardage. Forgive me for the yardage I unrolled today. Amen.

Initiative

The man without
a wedding garment
was thrown out
on his ear
from the great feast
   and the king
   was insulted
   by his presence.
My garment
has worn badly
through the years
and is tattered
at the edges.

My faith
has been rubbed
thin in spots
with blemish
showing through.

I am relieved to hear
an open invitation
from my King
   and to see
   that every time
   I come to the
   great feast
   a new robe
   is supplied.

I have but
to wear it.

My robe of faith is not always attractive, Lord, and you
seem to know when it needs a good Clorox whitening
now and then. Thank you for your open invitation and for
the lavish gift of renewal. All I need do is accept it.
Amen.

The two were unaware
that Christ walked with them
on the Emmaus road
and only knew it
when they sat at table
and he broke bread with them.
  There was something
  telling
  in that gesture.

Be present at our table, Lord

I wonder how often
I have walked an Emmaus road
and never knew
my Lord had walked with me.

I wonder if
my conversation
skimmed the surface
without knowing
that he probed
for depth.

But then—
how would I know?
  God has never
  broken bread
  or sipped the wine
  at my table—
  I think.

I want you at my table, Lord, but many times our
conversations and arguments keep you out. I want you
at the center of my family, but we jet in so many
directions it seems all but impossible to zero in on you.
Don't let us go! Hold us together and hold us to you,
that our walking and talking and eating might be in your
presence and that we might have the perception
to see you with us. Amen.

The young man
from Nain
arose from his death
at the bidding of Christ
and was returned
to his mother.

Mayor's holiday

The words of Jesus
caused a miracle to happen
and God's power swept through
that little town.

The man was changed
perceptibly
    and maybe
    all of Nain
    was changed
    as well.

I hope the mayor
declared a holiday!

I am slow to celebrate the good things in my life, Lord,
but do my share of complaining over the rough spots.
Let my joy erupt in undeclared holidays with my family
to give us all more time and space to see your goodness
and to sing a song of thanksgiving. Amen.

A little servant girl
brought Naaman
to the river
of God's love—
  a Naaman
  whose chariots
  and power
  carried out
  his bidding
but could not
carry him
to God.

Naaman found
his prestige
mattered little
  but the turning
  of his heart
  to God was
  paramount.

He was healed
in spite of pomp
and circumstance
  because a little
  servant girl
  invited him
  to know
  her Lord.

Sharing

Lord, help me to see the importance of invitations—
winsome invitations to invite others to know you, to
discover your presence in their lives. I am caught up in
formalities so often and need to be reminded of
simplicity—the simple act of coming to you and
bringing someone with me. Amen.

Simon and Andrew
were fishing
when Jesus
caught them
to a new life
and told them
to fish for people.

Singleness of purpose

Perhaps they wondered
at the bait to use
until they walked
with him awhile
and felt the power
of his love
   and knew the
   strength of it
   was greater far
   than fishing nets
   and the beauty of it
   unsurpassed by
   rolling seas.

They turned away—
forsaking seas
and fishing nets
to follow Christ.

O God, I need to get away. I'm engulfed in responsibilities in church, community, and home. I resent
intrusion on my time and abilities. Help me to know
when I can forsake my fish and get about the business
of following you. Maybe I can't forsake anything at all,
but need a firmer grip on you in the same old pattern
of my days. Simon and Andrew knew the difference.
Help me to know it also. Amen.

Noah sent a bird
into a wilderness
of sea and sky
to test the promise
of the Lord
   and waited
   for its winged returning
   and a leaf.

Answer
pending

I have sent
a tester from
my wilderness
of doubt because
   my little craft
   requires mooring
   in a new day
   of unchartered sea
and he promised
to be the anchor.

I wait
for my bird
with the sprig
of green.

I may be pushing, God, but I need some direct answers
today. Sometimes a small miracle is in order to give
a clear set of direction, and this is one of those times.
Please give me a sign, that I may know with certainty
this is the road you would have me walk. There are
several others I'd rather be traveling. Amen.

81

Jesus healed
with little more provocation
than a need announced—
    the blind man
    the leper
    the paralytic.

Help me to help

Their cries were not
from holy men
but from sick ones.
He didn't ask their
    lineage
    military status
    bank account
    insurance plan
but heard their cry
and healed them
indiscriminately.

God, help me to be as indiscriminate in my ministry
to people as you, so that I might respond to need
whenever it is and whoever it is—even when the word
"help" isn't used. Amen.

Fresh joy

Ten lepers
were cleansed
of disease
   and rejoiced
   in new wholeness
   of body.

One leper
returned
in thanksgiving
   and lay his joy
   at the feet
   of Jesus.

His body
was clean
and his spirit
sang a new song
   that was
   lifted
   on wings
   of gratitude.

I would be cleansed
of body and soul.
I would receive
a mind newly grateful
and a joy
to lay
at his feet.

Oh! Thank you for life that is made beautiful and clean
through you. Thank you for mountaintops of joy that
rise high in sunlight and laughter, for the music of
friendship whose harmonies are sweet, for the strength
to walk with vigor in my world, and for love that
encompasses it all. Thank you for health of body this day.
Amen.

83

Jesus labeled
teachers of the Law
and Pharisees
    imposters!

He was not quiet
in his wrath,
but spelled out
their hypocrisy with
    "Blind fools!
    How blind you are!
    Whitewashed tombs
    with rotten stuff
    inside."

He made enemies
    because he dared
    to rock the boat
    with justice
    and mercy
    and honesty
until the religious
appeared as scoundrels
in the light
of his truth.

Their pious masks
were torn
from naked faces
and they stood
revealed.

It was not easy
for them to
stand naked
before God
    and they hated
    the truth
    of his words.

Pious masks

It is not easy
for me to
stand naked
before God
    but he knows
    my nakedness
    and clothes me
    with his love.

I am not better than those Pharisees, Lord, but I hate to admit it. I spend precious time worrying about what other people think and trying to wear the right mask for the right occasion. I can't seem to be independent of the opinion of others. Maybe it isn't even necessary. But I'd like to be more myself than a pretense of something I'm not.

Help me to live honestly with myself and others, Lord, so I can be a growing person, open to changes and open to your will for me. Amen.

Peter jumped
out of his boat
and nearly drowned—
    the fool!

The blithering idiot
had the notion
he could walk on water
    and all but perished
    when he tried.

Jesus held his hand
and saved his pride
    and also perhaps his life.

Jesus loved the brash act
of a man
who threw caution
to the winds
in one wild
impulsive moment
and went overboard
for his Lord.

Social insecurity

Lord, let me leave the security of my little boat. Give
me courage to go overboard and walk on uncertain waters
for you. Fling your life jacket of hope onto deep waves,
that my feet may move with a little less caution over
perilous depths. Amen.

The man was
deaf and dumb
when Jesus touched
his ears
his tongue
and set him free.

Unawareness

The ears
could not hear
and the tongue
could not speak
    until the power of God
    burst the silence with sound
    and rushed an eloquence
    to tardy lips.

I solicit
the same power
for my ears
that need to hear
the voice of God
and my tongue
that needs to
speak of God—
    and the delicate
    surgery of release
    from the bondage
    of unawareness.

At times I hear without knowing what you say, Lord,
and strain to understand without really wanting to. I am
ashamed of my indifference and shocked by my
carelessness. The deaf and dumb have nothing on me!
I walk impervious to signs of your leading along the way.
I jog contentedly in my own rut. Give me a painful
disturbance to my complacency, and sharp awareness
of you. Amen.

The tickets must be sold.
  Today I have been
  in the business of selling
  for my church
  (always with a smile)
  to somehow prove that
  I am a good citizen
  and very much a Christian.

I can't stop running

The book must be read.
  This is my book club day
  and everyone knows
  we must keep up
  with current trends
  and the stimulating thought
  of our contemporaries.

This is my luncheon day.
  The girls will miss me
  if I do not show
  and the speaker will be inspirational,
  encouraging me to become
  a better person and
  most surely
  a better Christian.

God must find
this hectic pace discouraging
when all he wants
is my undivided attention
so that he can
get through to me.

I know that when
he does get through
I won't be nearly
so busy proving myself
a good citizen
and a worthy Christian.

For he has broken
through before
and touched me
with his power.

Then I have been released
to be his person
　　unencumbered with
　　the business of
　　pushing me
but ready to be
vulnerable
for him.

　I'm on a merry-go-round, Lord, and I don't know how
to get off. There aren't enough hours in the day to
finish the good things I start. After all, you want me to be
a responsible person.
　But my schedule is so full I can't seem to find time
for my family anymore, or for you. I guess I feel
indispensable to my garden club (you're in favor of
flowers), my bridge club (we've been together since
girlhood), my book discussion group (for broadening my
mind), my bowling league (I owe myself some recreation),
my church circle (I must do something for my
congregation).
　What's the matter with me? I've lost sight of your
value system and I'm running wild with mine. Forgive my
frenetic haste and busyness. Stop me! Stop me! Help me
remember that you come first, and show me how
to keep you there. Amen.

She only touched
the fringe
of his robe
to be
made well
   but she did touch.

She reached out
to him
in her need
and found
healing.

He reached out
to her
from his strength
and made
whole.

Together
they reached
for a miracle
and found it—
   the miracle
   of seeing God
   in each other.

Tangible evidence

I reach for you, God, in the days and nights when I, too,
need to touch the fringe of your robe and be made
whole. I forget at times that you are reaching for me even
before I articulate my need. Let me remember that you
are always present and ready to heal my body, spirit,
mind. Let me also remember that you expect me to
expect the healing and to reach for it. Amen.

The death of Lazarus
brought a miracle
of resurrection
as Jesus called him
from a silent grave
and freed him
from the shroud.

Out of the old cocoon

A butterfly emerges
from its dark cocoon
    winged
    unshackled
    beautiful.

I wonder if Lazarus
dragged his feet
as he returned
to the old cocoon
    just after he had
    stepped unshackled
    on that other shore.

Forgive me if it is unseemly, Lord, but I've always
wondered what Lazarus felt about being returned to this
earth and whether he was very happy to be back in the
old cocoon of this life. I guess this miracle was for Mary
and Martha and their friends—not Lazarus—wasn't it?

I do a lot of fussing and fretting in my old cocoon,
Lord, and at times I can scarcely wait to be free of this
shackled life and its limitations. But there are other times
when I feel like the butterfly—winged and free—and life
is rich and beautiful. At such times I am more aware of
you and your love and more open to the giving
and receiving of love around me.

Help me get out of my old cocoon more often. Amen.

Please and thank you
are the words
we've all been taught to say,
and we have learned
our lessons well,
for when we bow to pray,
it's "Please, dear Lord,
it's I, dear Lord,
who need your help again.
Do lift this burden
from my back,
and thanks, dear Lord. Amen."

Stifled prayer

Lord,
stewardship drives
drive me up the wall
    hurrying
    scurrying
    plotting
    planning
strategies to secure support
for an already pared budget
from people who
resent intrusion
into private purses.

I am ashamed
we find it necessary
to solicit in your name.

And I am ashamed
that we must
plead your cause
before a congregation
boasting two-car garages
and color TVs.

Since when
has giving
become
    a duty
    instead of
    a privilege
a drag
instead of
a joy
    a bore
    instead of
    a blessing?

I know—
    since the beginning
    of time.

Stewardship drives

Maybe we should stop
dramatizing needs
in high rhetoric
    and just
    ask for money!

No
hero buttons

Sometimes
I look for
hero buttons
Lord
and am surprised
to find your
lack of accolades.

It is not
amusing
to discern
your spartan
expectations
    and it is not
    comforting
    to bear
    a heavy conscience
and it is not
levitating
to be made
aware.

On the other hand
Lord
    save your
    hero buttons
    for heroes!

Disposables

Today my life
seems disposable
  like the empty
  milk carton
  on the breakfast table.

The problem is—
  who will stamp me flat
  and throw me out?

Today's culture
forbids such littering
  despite the
  obscenities
  of Dachau
and the death
trenches of
My Lai.

Besides,
  tomorrow
  my life's carton
  may be full to
  overflowing
and the disposable
quite indispensable
after all.

Lord,
   hold her
   in your love today
   and let her know
   the beauty of your presence.

She is lonely,
and even with
my arms around her
she knows that sometime
they will not be enough
and that she must
travel on alone.

But for now
let my arms
hold her for you
and my love
surround her
in your name
   that when you
   lift her to
   that other shore
   she will step quickly
   without fear
   and smile hello.

Prayer for a dying friend

I thought I knew
the Christ
until he crashed
my private door
well marked
"Keep Out."

Private loss

I thought we had
a good rapport
until I came aware
of his first
requirement—
myself!

I thought we had
an understanding
before he shook
my neat complacency
and crumbled my defenses
in the dust.

If I should choose
to know him better
it will be at risk
of losing me.

I do not know
if I can chance
such losing.

But
if in losing me
I find the Christ—
   on such a promise
   I will stake
   my life!

Okay, God,
   with the vacuum running
   I can shout
   and not be heard
   by anyone but you.

Today I must shout
   because you haven't
   answered my prayers lately
   and they have been
   good prayers
   and reasonable
   and not altogether
   selfish.

I can't believe your answer
   was a downright "no"
   and I've been looking
   in all the right places
   for some sign
   to show me
   you heard and
   you are working
   on it.

I am presumptuous enough
   to think you
   do not expect me
   to wait forever!

I am hanging on
to all the promises
held out in
your book:
   "Ask—you will receive."
   "Seek—and you will find."
   "Knock—it will be opened."
   "Let your requests be made known."
But I am weary

Vacuum cleaner conversation

of hanging on
and I am tired to death
  of seeking and not finding
  of knocking and not opening
  and of letting my requests
  be known to you
  in big silences.

So now I'm yelling, God,
  in my own house
  uncluttered with people
  but alive to the
  noisy vacuum cleaner.
  And I know you hear
  in spite of all
  this racket
  and in spite
  of me.

There! I've turned it off!
  What was that
  you said?

God,
I missed you
in church
this morning
because
    I was busy
    worrying about
    the high G
    and tempo change
    of our anthem—
    to say nothing
    of the Latin,
    which was a stranger
    to my bumbling tongue
    and staggered forth
    with heavy step,
    even in pianissimo.
I missed you
because I
was caught up
in resentment over
back-row chitchat
    and because
    the dull mechanics
    of a liturgy
    had grown too familiar
    with apathetic use.
Our soprano section
was noticeably thin
and our director
was noticeably worried
and our voices
raised to your glory
were noticeably amateur.
Yet
here is the
irony—
    we sing to your glory

Lamentations
(of a choir member)

in your house of worship
but miss the glory
because we are stifled
in the tension of performance
against a measurement
of obscure critics
and forget that
you are loving us
through high Gs
and lumbering Latin
and that you want
a great crescendo
from our hearts
that has nothing
to do with
notation or musicology
    but lifts
    a magnificent
    hymn of praise
    to you.
You were not
absent, Lord—
    I was—
and my choir robe covered
an uptight soprano
more than a rousing worshiper.

I now have
one less hang-up
Lord—
     the one that says
     our home will
     meet the standard
     of spotless perfection
     should a visitor
     drop in.

I love drop-ins
Lord,
for they are
the leaven of my life.
They bring their
laughter
tears
dailiness
     and very little
     perfection
to our doorstep.

Thank you
for newly giving me
a blind spot to
     papers
     pillows
     dust-balls
in favor of
friendship and
the intangibles
of love.

One less hang-up

A mother is, after all,
only a human being,
and today I cannot cope
with three other human beings
who are also my children.

My teenage daughter
wants to be fired-up
about her religion
    and since this is not
    one of my fired-up days
    I cannot ignite the tinder
    of her soul.

But God, you can.
You can hold her
in your love today
and spark the tender flame of faith
that is a part of her
until it leaps into
a burst of light
that she can feel
and translate with your nearness.

At the same time, Lord,
let me show her
that even on unfired days
you are present too,
    stoking our faith
    against the needs of our souls
    and making a long-term
    investment in our
    ordinary living.

And I am concerned about
our not-quite-teenage son
who is so afraid of losing
he will not try to win
and whose little confidence

I can't cope

magnifies his fear
and stifles his self-awareness.

How to let him know
I am supporting him
without handing out
a pair of crutches
on which to hobble
or a love that consumes
more than it frees?

And our youngest son,
whose robust swagger
turns me off at times
and whose arrogance
raises my blood pressure.

How to let him know
my love is sure and steady
without his proving anything?

A mother is, after all,
only a human being,
and today I cannot cope
with these other human needs
    and I ask
    an immense portion
    of your help
    to see me through
    and to see them through
    these growing years.

(Would it surprise them
to know
I am still growing?)

Prognosis

I know my organs
are in order
and each is functioning
according to plan
for I have submitted
once again to being
   poked
   pounded
   pressurized
until no part of me
has escaped the
discerning eye
of my doctor.

The blood is flowing
richly through veins
showing
   hemoglobin high
   cholesterol low
   blood count normal
and I am content
to know my body
sings of health.

But what of my soul?
What of that yearning
growing part of me
that reaches for God
in the daytime of joy
and the night of despair?

What of the extravagant self
that spills out to others
   or the creeping
   crawling thing
   that hides
   in a hole of
   its own misery?
What of the

flaming rocket
of love that soars
   and the gray
   stone of hate
   that sinks?
O God!
Put me under the microscope
of your tender scrutiny
and the X ray
of your love
and measure me
against the giving
of your Son
   for in him
   I have
   a perfect
   wholeness
and in him
my prognosis is:
LOVED.

I'm tired
of listening
Lord
and I am
   sodden
   sopped and
   saturated
with the troubles
of other people.

I'm tired

Doesn't anyone
see my need
to ventilate and let go
my feelings stored neatly
on a shelf marked "Fragile"?

Doesn't anyone
see my need
to shout
and weep?

Doesn't anyone
see my need
to rant
and rave?

Doesn't anyone
see my need
to complain
   or my bid
   for sympathy?

My ears reverberate
and my mind resounds
   with real troubles
   of real people
   in a real world.
When will the real world
discover I too am real?

Dear God, last night was long for me.
I could not sleep. I seemed to see
the faces of your children there
against the darkness everywhere.
    The hungry ones
        the crying ones
            the sick ones
                and the dying ones.
Their little faces haunt me yet
Into the day. I can't forget.

**An
open
letter
to God**

Forgive me please, but I would know
why these small ones must suffer so,
caught helpless in a world of men
who make a living hell for them.
    Forgive me please,
        but on my knees
            I cry for these,
                I cry for these,
the children who are tired and worn,
who did not ask us to be born.

Perhaps the hours will hold the song
of a small child who runs along
the edges of my world today.
But for the others, Lord, I pray—
    for hungry ones
        for crying ones
            for sick ones
                and for dying ones.
You healed the sick, the blind, the lame.
Oh! let me love them in your name!

"You were too troubled, child, to sleep?
Then feed these little ones . . . my sheep."